Bev and Lil

Written by Camille Josephine Carr

Illustrations by Lela Meunier

Archway Publishing books may be ordered through booksellers or by contacting:

Archway Publishing
1663 Liberty Drive
Bloomington, IN 47403
www.archwaypublishing.com
844.669.3957

Illustrations by Lela Meunier

ISBN: 978-1-4808-9547-8 (sc)
ISBN: 978-1-4808-9546-1 (hc)
ISBN: 978-1-4808-9548-5 (e)

Print information available on the last page.

Archway Publishing rev. date: 10/22/2020

DEDICATION

This book is dedicated to all the families who find joy and magic and beauty in what is possible.

Once there were two sisters
named Bev and Lil.

Lil was little and wild. She
liked kicking balls and playing
in the muck.

Bev was big and mild. She liked reading books and rolling her eyes.

But Lil loved Bev.

Nothing could ever change the love Bev and Lil had for each other. It was unending, unwavering, and unconditional.

They liked to sing loud and dance proud. They liked to make messes and wear pretty dresses.

And Bev loved Lil.

But some things would change when Lil got sick. Lil's sickness was a thief. It stole until Lil almost had nothing left. Until wild, willful Lil became too sick to walk and too sick to talk.

There was nothing that her
doctors could do.

They knew that Lil did not have enough time left. Bev and Lil knew this too, so they decided to use that time well.

They sang and danced differently.
But it was still quite loud and still
very proud.

They made more messes and wore even prettier dresses. Silly girl Lil could no longer run, but she still had the most fun.

Along the way, Bev and Lil
made many friends.

Friends who painted
Lil's nails.

And braided
Lil's hair.

Friends who played
music for Lil and

Friends who made
Lil laugh.

Lil had many good days with her friends but she also had a few not-so-good days. Sometimes she was tired. Sometimes she was sick. And sometimes she was angry.

But Lil was never alone and she was never truly unhappy. The life Lil lived was never easy but it was never empty.

The love Lil was given was unending, unwavering and unconditional and so was the love she gave back.

Bev loved Lil and Lil loved Bev. Lil loved her life and she lived it well.

About the author:

Camille Josephine Carr is a student at the College of Wooster, where she majors in sociology. She lives outside of Philadelphia. This is her first book.

About the Illustrator:

Lela Meunier earned her BFA from the Tyler School of Art. She is an educator and illustrator who lives in Williamstown, Massachusetts.

The book was made possible with the support of The Calliope Joy Foundation and the Pennsylvania Pediatric Palliative Care Coalition.

The book is inspired by the palliative care and pediatric hospice nurses, therapists, aides, and doctors who care for children and support their families.

All the author royalties from book sales will support the Kind Pediatric Hospice Program (Abington Hospital—Jefferson Health) and the Pediatric Advanced Care Team at the Children's Hospital of Philadelphia.